Copyright © 2023 by S. J. Matthews (Author)

This book is protected by copyright law and is intended solely for personal use. Reproduction, distribution, or any other form of use requires the written permission of the author. The information presented in this book is for educational and entertainment purposes only, and while every effort has been made to ensure its accuracy and completeness, no guarantees are made. The author is not providing legal, financial, medical, or professional advice, and readers should consult with a licensed professional before implementing any of the techniques discussed in this book. The content in this book has been sourced from various reliable sources, but readers should exercise their own judgment when using this information. The author is not responsible for any losses, direct or indirect, that may occur from the use of this book, including but not limited to errors, omissions, or inaccuracies.

We hope this book has been informative and helpful on your journey to understanding and celebrating older adults. Thank you for your interest and support!

Title: 51% Attacks and the Future of Blockchain Security
Subtitle: An Introduction

Series: Defending Bitcoin: A Comprehensive Guide to 51% Attack Prevention

By S. J. Matthews

"Bitcoin is a remarkable cryptographic achievement and the ability to create something that is not duplicable in the digital world has enormous value."
Eric Schmidt, Former CEO of Google

"Bitcoin is a technological tour de force."
Bill Gates, Co-Founder of Microsoft

"Bitcoin is the beginning of something great: a currency without a government, something necessary and imperative."
Nassim Taleb, Author of "The Black Swan"

"Bitcoin is a remarkable cryptographic achievement... The ability to create something which is not duplicable in the digital world has enormous value."
Roger Ver, Bitcoin Investor and Entrepreneur

"Bitcoin is a remarkable cryptographic achievement and the ability to create something that is not duplicable in the digital world has enormous value."

Peter Thiel, Co-Founder of PayPal

"Bitcoin is a very exciting development, it might lead to a world currency. I think over the next decade it will grow to become one of the most important ways to pay for things and transfer assets."
Kim Dotcom, Founder of Megaupload

"Bitcoin is a protocol that could change the world, like the web did. Don't miss out."
Andreas Antonopoulos, Bitcoin Educator and Author

"Bitcoin is better than currency in that you don't have to be physically in the same place and, of course, for large transactions, currency can get pretty inconvenient."
Bill Gates, Co-Founder of Microsoft

Table of Contents

Introduction 7
  Overview of blockchain technology 7
  Brief introduction to 51% attacks 10
  Importance of preventing 51% attacks 12

Chapter 1: "What are 51% Attacks 15
  Explanation of 51% attacks 15
  Types of 51% attacks 17
  History of 51% attacks in cryptocurrencies 20

Chapter 2: "How do 51% Attacks Work? 23
  Technical explanation of 51% attacks 23
  Steps involved in a 51% attack 26
  Common vulnerabilities exploited in 51% attacks 29

Chapter 3: "The Impact of 51% Attacks 33
  Consequences of successful 51% attacks 33
  Examples of the impact of 51% attacks on blockchain ecosystems 37
  Why preventing 51% attacks is crucial for the growth of blockchain technology 41

Chapter 4: "Preventing 51% Attacks 45

Strategies for preventing 51% attacks 45
Comparison of proof-of-work and proof-of-stake mechanisms... 51
Other prevention techniques, such as sharding and cross-chain interoperability... 54

Conclusion 56
Summary of key takeaways.. 56
Call to action for preventing 51% attacks...................... 58

Key Terms and Definitions 61
Supporting Materials... 63

Introduction

Overview of blockchain technology

Blockchain technology is the backbone of cryptocurrencies such as Bitcoin. It is a distributed ledger that records and verifies transactions in a secure and transparent manner. In this chapter, we'll provide an overview of blockchain technology, including its history, key features, and benefits.

History of Blockchain Technology

Blockchain technology was first introduced in 2008 as a component of the Bitcoin protocol by an unknown person or group of people using the pseudonym Satoshi Nakamoto. It was designed to solve the problem of double-spending, which is a common issue with digital currencies. The first Bitcoin transaction was recorded on January 3, 2009, marking the birth of blockchain technology.

Key Features of Blockchain Technology

The key features of blockchain technology include decentralization, immutability, and transparency. Decentralization means that there is no central authority or middleman controlling the network. Instead, all participants in the network have an equal say in the validation and verification of transactions. Immutability refers to the fact that once a transaction is recorded on the blockchain, it cannot be altered or deleted. This makes the blockchain an ideal solution for storing sensitive data and conducting secure transactions. Finally, transparency means that all transactions are visible to all participants in the network, providing an extra layer of security and accountability.

Benefits of Blockchain Technology

Blockchain technology has several benefits, including increased security, improved efficiency, and reduced costs. Because blockchain transactions are secure and immutable, they are resistant to fraud and hacking attempts. This makes blockchain technology ideal for industries such as finance, healthcare, and supply chain management. Blockchain technology also reduces the need for intermediaries, which can result in faster transactions and lower costs.

Conclusion

Blockchain technology is a powerful tool that has the potential to revolutionize the way we conduct transactions and store data. It provides increased security, improved efficiency, and reduced costs, making it ideal for a wide range of applications. In the next chapter, we'll explore the concept of 51% attacks and how they can compromise the security of blockchain networks like Bitcoin.

Brief introduction to 51% attacks

51% attacks are a major threat to the security of blockchain networks like Bitcoin. In this chapter, we'll provide a brief introduction to 51% attacks, including what they are, how they work, and why they are a concern for the Bitcoin community.

What are 51% Attacks?

A 51% attack occurs when a group of miners or nodes on a blockchain network controls more than 50% of the network's computing power. This gives them the ability to control the network and manipulate transactions. In the case of Bitcoin, this means that the attackers could potentially double-spend coins or rewrite the entire blockchain.

How do 51% Attacks Work?

To carry out a 51% attack, the attackers must first gain control of the majority of the network's computing power. This can be done by either recruiting a large number of miners or by renting or buying computing power from cloud providers. Once they control the majority of the computing power, the attackers can begin to manipulate transactions by either excluding certain transactions or reversing transactions that have already been confirmed.

Why are 51% Attacks a Concern?

51% attacks are a major concern for the Bitcoin community because they can compromise the security and integrity of the network. If an attacker successfully carries out a 51% attack, they can potentially steal coins or manipulate transactions, which can undermine the trust in the entire network. Additionally, the cost of carrying out a 51% attack has decreased over time, making it easier for attackers to carry out such an attack.

Conclusion

In conclusion, 51% attacks are a major threat to the security of blockchain networks like Bitcoin. They can compromise the integrity of the network and undermine the trust in the entire system. In the next chapter, we'll provide a more detailed explanation of 51% attacks, including the different types that exist and how they can be prevented.

Importance of preventing 51% attacks

The security of blockchain networks like Bitcoin is essential to maintain the trust and integrity of the system. 51% attacks can pose a significant threat to the security of these networks, and preventing them is of utmost importance. In this chapter, we'll explore why preventing 51% attacks is critical for the continued growth and adoption of blockchain technology.

The Impact of Successful 51% Attacks

If a 51% attack is successful, the consequences can be severe. Attackers can double-spend coins, manipulate transactions, and rewrite the entire blockchain. This can result in significant financial losses for users and can undermine the trust in the network, leading to decreased adoption and usage.

Furthermore, a successful 51% attack can have a ripple effect on the entire cryptocurrency ecosystem. Other cryptocurrencies may also be affected if attackers are able to exploit the same vulnerabilities that were used to carry out the attack on the Bitcoin network.

Preventing 51% Attacks

Preventing 51% attacks is crucial to maintaining the security and integrity of blockchain networks. There are several ways to prevent these attacks, including:

1. Increasing the Hash Rate - One way to prevent 51% attacks is to increase the hash rate of the network. This can be done by adding more nodes or miners to the network, making it more difficult for attackers to control the majority of the computing power.

2. Implementing Consensus Mechanisms - Blockchain networks can implement consensus mechanisms like proof-of-stake or delegated proof-of-stake that make it more difficult for attackers to control the majority of the network's computing power.

3. Regularly Monitoring the Network - Regularly monitoring the network for signs of a potential 51% attack can help prevent such attacks before they occur.

4. Implementing Multi-Layer Security Measures - Blockchain networks can implement multi-layer security measures, such as sharding or cross-chain interoperability, to make it more difficult for attackers to manipulate the network.

Conclusion

In conclusion, preventing 51% attacks is essential to maintaining the security and integrity of blockchain networks like Bitcoin. The consequences of a successful attack can be severe and can undermine the trust in the entire system. Implementing various security measures can help prevent 51% attacks and ensure the continued growth and adoption of blockchain technology. In the following chapters, we'll explore the different types of 51% attacks, how they work, and the strategies for preventing them in more detail.

Chapter 1: "What are 51% Attacks

Explanation of 51% attacks

Before we can explore how to prevent 51% attacks, we first need to understand what they are and how they work. In this chapter, we'll dive into the details of 51% attacks and explore the different types of attacks that can occur.

What are 51% Attacks?

A 51% attack is a type of attack on a blockchain network where an attacker gains control of the majority of the network's computing power or hash rate. With this control, the attacker can manipulate the network's transactions, double-spend coins, and even rewrite the entire blockchain.

Types of 51% Attacks

There are two main types of 51% attacks: selfish mining and majority mining attacks.

1. Selfish Mining - In a selfish mining attack, the attacker creates a separate branch of the blockchain that is kept hidden from the rest of the network. When the attacker's branch becomes longer than the main branch, the attacker reveals their branch, which causes the main branch

to be discarded. This allows the attacker to double-spend coins and manipulate transactions.

2. Majority Mining - In a majority mining attack, the attacker gains control of the majority of the network's computing power. With this control, the attacker can manipulate transactions, double-spend coins, and even rewrite the entire blockchain.

History of 51% Attacks in Cryptocurrencies

51% attacks have been carried out on several blockchain networks, including Bitcoin, Ethereum Classic, and Verge. One of the most significant 51% attacks occurred in 2018 on the Ethereum Classic network, where attackers were able to double-spend coins worth over $1 million.

Conclusion

In conclusion, 51% attacks are a significant threat to the security and integrity of blockchain networks. Attackers can use their majority control of the network's computing power to manipulate transactions, double-spend coins, and rewrite the entire blockchain. In the following chapters, we'll explore the technical details of how 51% attacks work and the vulnerabilities that attackers can exploit.

Types of 51% attacks

As we discussed in the previous section, 51% attacks are a type of attack on a blockchain network where an attacker gains control of the majority of the network's computing power or hash rate. In this section, we'll explore the two main types of 51% attacks in more detail: selfish mining and majority mining attacks.

1. Selfish Mining

In a selfish mining attack, the attacker creates a separate branch of the blockchain that is kept hidden from the rest of the network. The attacker then continues to mine blocks on their branch, hoping that it will eventually become longer than the main branch.

Once the attacker's branch becomes longer than the main branch, the attacker reveals their branch to the rest of the network. This causes the main branch to be discarded, and the network accepts the attacker's branch as the new main branch.

By controlling the longest branch of the blockchain, the attacker can manipulate transactions and even double-spend coins. For example, the attacker can send a transaction on the main branch, then quickly switch to their own branch and send the same coins to a different address. Because the attacker's branch is longer, the network will accept it as the valid branch, and the double-spent coins will be considered valid.

Selfish mining attacks are difficult to detect because the attacker's branch is kept hidden until it becomes longer than the main branch. However, they require a significant amount of computing power to be successful.

2. Majority Mining

In a majority mining attack, the attacker gains control of the majority of the network's computing power. With this control, the attacker can manipulate transactions, double-spend coins, and even rewrite the entire blockchain.

To carry out a majority mining attack, the attacker needs to control more than 50% of the network's computing power. This gives them the ability to control the majority of the blocks that are added to the blockchain.

Once the attacker has control of the majority of the blocks, they can start manipulating transactions and even double-spending coins. For example, the attacker can send a transaction on the main blockchain, then quickly create a new branch of the blockchain that doesn't include that transaction. This allows the attacker to spend the same coins twice.

Majority mining attacks are much more difficult to carry out than selfish mining attacks because they require a significant amount of computing power. However, they are also much more dangerous because they can completely destroy the integrity of the blockchain.

Conclusion

In conclusion, there are two main types of 51% attacks: selfish mining and majority mining attacks. Selfish mining attacks involve creating a separate branch of the blockchain and manipulating transactions on that branch. Majority mining attacks involve gaining control of the majority of the network's computing power and manipulating transactions and the blockchain itself. Both types of attacks are significant threats to the security and integrity of blockchain networks, and in the next chapter, we'll explore the technical details of how these attacks work.

History of 51% attacks in cryptocurrencies

The first known 51% attack on a cryptocurrency blockchain occurred on June 13, 2014, on the Bitcoin alternative cryptocurrency, Peercoin. This event raised concerns about the security of blockchain networks, and since then, many cryptocurrencies have fallen victim to 51% attacks. In this chapter, we will examine the history of 51% attacks in cryptocurrencies, including the most notable attacks that have occurred.

1. The First 51% Attack

As mentioned, the first known 51% attack occurred on the Peercoin blockchain in June 2014. An unknown attacker gained control of more than 51% of the computing power on the network and began mining blocks at a faster rate than the rest of the network. This allowed the attacker to create their own blockchain fork, effectively double-spending coins they already owned on the network.

2. The Ethereum Classic Attack

One of the most well-known 51% attacks occurred on the Ethereum Classic blockchain in January 2019. The attacker gained control of more than 51% of the network's computing power and was able to perform a double-spend attack, stealing over $1 million worth of cryptocurrency. The attack caused widespread concern within the Ethereum Classic community, and there was a debate about whether the network should hard fork to prevent further attacks.

3. The Verge Attack

The Verge cryptocurrency network fell victim to a 51% attack in April 2018. The attacker exploited a vulnerability in the network's mining algorithm, which allowed them to mine blocks at an accelerated rate. They were able to double-spend more than $1.7 million worth of cryptocurrency before the network's developers implemented a hard fork to prevent further attacks.

4. The Bitcoin Gold Attack

In May 2018, the Bitcoin Gold cryptocurrency network was hit by a 51% attack. The attacker gained control of more than 51% of the network's computing power and was able to double-spend more than $18 million worth of cryptocurrency. The attack prompted the Bitcoin Gold community to implement a hard fork to prevent similar attacks in the future.

5. Other 51% Attacks

Other notable 51% attacks include those on the ZenCash and Monacoin networks in 2018, the Feathercoin network in 2013, and the Bitcoin Cash network in 2020. Each of these attacks caused varying degrees of damage to the networks and highlighted the importance of preventing 51% attacks.

6. Conclusion

The history of 51% attacks in cryptocurrencies shows that no network is immune to such attacks. As the value of cryptocurrencies continues to rise, so does the incentive for attackers to exploit vulnerabilities in these networks. It is essential for developers and users to remain vigilant and implement measures to prevent such attacks from occurring in the future.

Chapter 2: "How do 51% Attacks Work?

Technical explanation of 51% attacks

A 51% attack is a type of attack that can occur on a blockchain network, where a single entity or group of entities controls more than 50% of the network's hash power. In this scenario, the attacker can essentially control the blockchain and manipulate transactions, allowing them to double-spend coins and reverse transactions. This can have serious implications for the security and integrity of the network.

To understand how a 51% attack works, it is important to first understand the mechanics of a blockchain network. A blockchain is a decentralized ledger of transactions that is maintained by a network of nodes. These nodes work together to validate transactions and add them to the blockchain in a process known as mining.

When a transaction is initiated on a blockchain, it is broadcast to the network and verified by multiple nodes. Once verified, it is added to a block, which is then added to the blockchain by a process of consensus. In the case of Bitcoin and other proof-of-work blockchains, this consensus is achieved through a process called mining.

Mining involves solving complex mathematical problems in order to add a new block to the blockchain. The first miner to solve the problem is rewarded with a block reward and any transaction fees associated with the transactions included in the block. In order to solve the problem, miners must expend computational power, or hash power, which is measured in hashes per second.

In a 51% attack, an attacker gains control of more than 50% of the network's hash power, allowing them to effectively control the blockchain. They can do this by either controlling a majority of the network's mining nodes or by using a large amount of computational power to outcompete other miners and gain control of the network.

Once an attacker has control of the network, they can begin to manipulate transactions. One of the most common methods of attack is known as a double-spend attack. In a double-spend attack, the attacker spends their coins on one transaction and then creates a competing transaction that spends the same coins to a different address. They then use their control of the network to ensure that the second transaction is included in the blockchain instead of the original transaction, effectively reversing the original transaction.

Another potential method of attack is known as a block-withholding attack. In this scenario, the attacker mines blocks but does not broadcast them to the network, effectively preventing other miners from adding blocks to the blockchain. This can allow the attacker to manipulate transactions and double-spend coins.

Overall, a 51% attack is a serious threat to the security and integrity of a blockchain network. It can have significant implications for the value of the cryptocurrency associated with the network, as well as for the trust that users have in the network itself. As such, it is important for blockchain developers and users to understand the technical details of these attacks and to take steps to prevent them from occurring.

Steps involved in a 51% attack

A 51% attack is a complex and sophisticated attack that requires a lot of technical knowledge and computational power to execute. In this chapter, we will explore the various steps involved in a 51% attack and how they are carried out.

Step 1: Obtaining Sufficient Hash Power

To carry out a 51% attack, an attacker needs to obtain enough hash power to control the majority of the network's mining power. This means that the attacker needs to have more computational power than the rest of the nodes on the network combined. The attacker can achieve this by either using their own mining equipment or by renting hash power from a mining pool.

Step 2: Creating a Private Fork

Once the attacker has obtained enough hash power, they can create a private fork of the blockchain. This involves creating a new chain that is not connected to the main blockchain. The attacker will use their hash power to mine new blocks on this private fork, effectively creating a new version of the blockchain.

Step 3: Double Spending

With a private fork in place, the attacker can now carry out double-spending attacks. In a double-spending attack, the attacker spends their coins on the legitimate blockchain while also spending the same coins on their private fork. Since the attacker controls the majority of the hash power, they can mine blocks on their private fork faster than the legitimate blockchain. This means that the attacker's version of the blockchain will become longer than the legitimate blockchain, making it the new valid chain.

Step 4: Releasing the Private Fork

Once the attacker has successfully carried out the double-spending attack, they can release their private fork to the network. The legitimate nodes on the network will recognize the attacker's version of the blockchain as the valid chain, and the double-spent coins will be accepted as valid transactions.

Step 5: Covering Their Tracks

To avoid detection, the attacker will need to cover their tracks by deleting any evidence of the private fork. This involves erasing any records of the private fork from their mining equipment and destroying any evidence of the attack.

Step 6: Profiting from the Attack

With the double-spent coins now accepted as valid transactions, the attacker can profit by selling the double-spent coins for another cryptocurrency or fiat currency. The attacker can repeat this process as many times as they like, effectively stealing coins from the legitimate users of the network.

In conclusion, carrying out a 51% attack involves a series of complex steps that require a lot of technical knowledge and computational power. While these attacks are rare, they pose a significant threat to the security and stability of blockchain networks. Understanding the steps involved in a 51% attack is crucial for preventing and defending against these attacks.

Common vulnerabilities exploited in 51% attacks

While a 51% attack on a blockchain network may seem like an impossible feat to achieve, there are a number of common vulnerabilities that attackers can exploit to carry out such an attack. In this section, we will explore some of the most common vulnerabilities that attackers use to carry out 51% attacks on blockchain networks.

1. Low hash rate The hash rate is the speed at which a mining node on a blockchain network is able to solve the cryptographic puzzles that are required to add a new block to the blockchain. A low hash rate means that there are fewer nodes on the network, which makes it easier for an attacker to gain control of 51% of the network's hash rate. This vulnerability is particularly common in newer blockchain networks that have not yet attracted a large number of miners.

2. Centralization Another common vulnerability in blockchain networks is centralization. If a large portion of the network's hash rate is controlled by a single entity, such as a mining pool or a group of miners working together, it becomes easier for an attacker to gain control of the

necessary 51% of the hash rate. This is because the attacker only needs to gain control of the centralized entity, rather than having to gain control of a large number of individual nodes.

3. Difficulty adjustment Most blockchain networks use a difficulty adjustment algorithm to ensure that the rate at which new blocks are added to the blockchain remains relatively constant over time. However, this algorithm can be exploited by attackers. If an attacker is able to gain control of a large portion of the network's hash rate, they can use this control to manipulate the difficulty adjustment algorithm. By artificially reducing the difficulty of the algorithm, the attacker can increase their chances of successfully adding new blocks to the blockchain.

4. Double spending Double spending is another vulnerability that can be exploited in a 51% attack. Double spending refers to the act of spending the same cryptocurrency twice. In a blockchain network, double spending is prevented by the fact that each transaction must be verified by a majority of the nodes on the network. However, if an attacker is able to gain control of 51% of the

network's hash rate, they can override the verification process and spend the same cryptocurrency twice.

5. Sybil attacks A Sybil attack is a type of attack in which an attacker creates multiple fake identities or nodes on a blockchain network in order to gain control of the network's hash rate. By controlling a large number of nodes on the network, the attacker can manipulate the network's verification process and carry out a 51% attack.

6. Time-based vulnerabilities Some blockchain networks have vulnerabilities that are time-based. For example, a network may have a block time that is too short, which makes it easier for an attacker to carry out a 51% attack. Alternatively, a network may have a block time that is too long, which makes the network less efficient and less secure overall.

Conclusion

While 51% attacks on blockchain networks are relatively rare, they do pose a significant threat to the security and stability of these networks. By exploiting common vulnerabilities in blockchain networks, attackers can gain control of the necessary 51% of the network's hash rate and carry out a variety of malicious activities, including double spending and block reorganization. To defend against 51% attacks, it is important for blockchain networks to be designed with security in mind and to implement measures to prevent centralization, low hash rates, and other common vulnerabilities.

Chapter 3: "The Impact of 51% Attacks

Consequences of successful 51% attacks

A successful 51% attack on a blockchain network can have significant consequences for the network and its users. In this section, we will discuss the various consequences of a successful 51% attack.

1. Double Spending

Double spending is the most common consequence of a successful 51% attack. In a double-spending attack, the attacker spends the same cryptocurrency twice by exploiting the blockchain's consensus mechanism. The attacker can do this by creating a fork in the blockchain, which allows them to control the majority of the network's hash rate. Once the attacker has control, they can execute transactions on their own forked chain and then release the original chain, which will overwrite the legitimate transactions with the double-spending transactions. This can result in significant financial losses for the affected parties.

2. Reorganization of the Blockchain

A successful 51% attack can result in the reorganization of the blockchain, which means that the attacker can rewrite the blockchain's history. The attacker can modify or delete previously recorded transactions and replace them with their own transactions. This can lead to the loss of trust in the blockchain network and its underlying technology.

3. Network Congestion

A 51% attack can also result in network congestion. The attacker can create a backlog of transactions by excluding legitimate transactions from the blockchain. This can cause delays in transaction confirmations and result in higher transaction fees for users who want their transactions to be processed quickly.

4. Loss of Confidence in the Network

A successful 51% attack can cause a loss of confidence in the blockchain network and its underlying technology. Users may lose faith in the network's security and may choose to avoid using it altogether, leading to a decline in the network's overall value and adoption.

5. Damage to Reputation

A successful 51% attack can damage the reputation of the affected blockchain network and its operators. This can lead to legal action, financial losses, and a decline in investor confidence. Moreover, it can create a negative perception of blockchain technology as a whole, leading to setbacks in its adoption and development.

6. Market Manipulation

A successful 51% attack can also lead to market manipulation. The attacker can manipulate the market by artificially inflating or deflating the price of the affected cryptocurrency. This can result in financial losses for investors who buy or sell the cryptocurrency at manipulated prices.

7. Loss of Resources

A 51% attack can result in the loss of resources for the blockchain network and its users. The attacker can consume a significant amount of computational power and energy to execute the attack, leading to higher operational costs and slower network performance.

In conclusion, a successful 51% attack can have significant consequences for the blockchain network and its users, including financial losses, network congestion, loss of confidence, damage to reputation, market manipulation, and loss of resources. Therefore, preventing 51% attacks is crucial for the growth and adoption of blockchain technology.

Examples of the impact of 51% attacks on blockchain ecosystems

In recent years, there have been several examples of successful 51% attacks on blockchain ecosystems. These attacks have caused significant damage to the affected networks and undermined confidence in the security and reliability of blockchain technology. In this section, we will discuss some of the most notable examples of 51% attacks and their impact on the blockchain ecosystem.

1. Ethereum Classic (ETC)

In January 2019, Ethereum Classic suffered a 51% attack that resulted in the theft of over $1 million worth of ETC. The attack was made possible by a combination of a lack of hashpower on the network and the availability of rental hashpower on NiceHash, a marketplace for hashpower. The attacker was able to double-spend ETC by creating a private chain, depositing ETC on exchanges, and then reversing the transaction by reorganizing the chain.

The attack caused a significant loss of confidence in Ethereum Classic, with some exchanges delisting the cryptocurrency and investors losing trust in its security. In response, the Ethereum Classic community proposed several solutions to prevent future attacks, including a modified proof-of-work algorithm and a move to a proof-of-stake consensus mechanism.

2. Verge (XVG)

In April 2018, Verge suffered a 51% attack that lasted for several hours and resulted in the theft of over $1.7 million worth of XVG. The attacker was able to exploit a vulnerability in Verge's mining algorithm that allowed them to manipulate the timestamp of blocks and make them easier to mine.

The attack caused a significant loss of confidence in Verge, with investors losing faith in its security and reliability. In response, the Verge community proposed several solutions to prevent future attacks, including a switch to a different mining algorithm and the implementation of new security features.

3. Bitcoin Gold (BTG)

In May 2018, Bitcoin Gold suffered a 51% attack that resulted in the theft of over $18 million worth of BTG. The attack was made possible by a combination of a lack of hashpower on the network and the availability of rental hashpower on NiceHash. The attacker was able to double-spend BTG by creating a private chain, depositing BTG on exchanges, and then reversing the transaction by reorganizing the chain.

The attack caused a significant loss of confidence in Bitcoin Gold, with some exchanges delisting the cryptocurrency and investors losing trust in its security. In response, the Bitcoin Gold community proposed several solutions to prevent future attacks, including a modified proof-of-work algorithm and a move to a proof-of-stake consensus mechanism.

4. Monacoin (MONA)

In May 2018, Monacoin suffered a 51% attack that lasted for several hours and resulted in the theft of over $90,000 worth of MONA. The attack was made possible by a combination of a lack of hashpower on the network and the availability of rental hashpower on NiceHash. The attacker was able to manipulate the mining difficulty of the network and carry out a double-spend attack.

The attack caused a significant loss of confidence in Monacoin, with some exchanges delisting the cryptocurrency and investors losing trust in its security. In response, the Monacoin community proposed several solutions to prevent future attacks, including a switch to a different mining algorithm and the implementation of new security features.

In conclusion, successful 51% attacks on blockchain ecosystems can have serious consequences for the affected networks, including loss of confidence in the technology, delisting by exchanges, and significant financial losses for investors. As such, preventing 51% attacks should be a top priority for the blockchain community, and efforts should be made to develop new security measures and consensus mechanisms to safeguard against these types of attacks.

Why preventing 51% attacks is crucial for the growth of blockchain technology

Blockchain technology has the potential to revolutionize industries, from finance to supply chain management, by offering secure, transparent, and decentralized systems that can improve efficiency, reduce costs, and enhance trust. However, blockchain networks, including the Bitcoin network, are not immune to attacks, and 51% attacks are among the most severe threats that can undermine the integrity and reliability of the entire system. Therefore, preventing 51% attacks is crucial for the growth and adoption of blockchain technology, and this chapter explains why.

Ensuring Security and Trust

One of the main advantages of blockchain technology is its security features, including cryptographic protocols, consensus mechanisms, and immutability, that make it difficult to alter or manipulate the data stored on the blockchain. However, these security features can be compromised by 51% attacks, which can enable attackers to rewrite the blockchain's history, double-spend coins, or exclude legitimate transactions from the network. Such attacks not only damage the immediate victims but also erode the trust and confidence in the entire blockchain network, as users may lose faith in the system's security and reliability.

Therefore, preventing 51% attacks is essential for ensuring the security and trust of blockchain networks. By implementing robust security measures and maintaining a decentralized and diverse network, blockchain networks can reduce the risk of 51% attacks and provide a secure and trustworthy environment for users to conduct transactions and store data.

Promoting Innovation and Investment

Blockchain technology has the potential to enable new business models, services, and products that can benefit various industries and economies. However, these innovations and investments require a stable and predictable blockchain environment that can support the growth and adoption of the technology. 51% attacks can disrupt this environment by causing uncertainty, volatility, and losses that can discourage users and investors from using or investing in the blockchain network.

Therefore, preventing 51% attacks is crucial for promoting innovation and investment in blockchain technology. By providing a secure and stable blockchain environment, users and investors can have more confidence in the technology's potential, and businesses can develop and launch new applications and services that can enhance their competitiveness and value.

Protecting Against Centralization and Monopoly

One of the key features of blockchain technology is its decentralized nature, which means that no single entity or authority controls the network, and all participants have equal rights and responsibilities. However, 51% attacks can undermine this decentralization by enabling a single entity or group to gain control of the network and dictate the rules and transactions on the blockchain. This centralization can lead to monopolies, censorship, and other forms of control that can erode the benefits of blockchain technology.

Therefore, preventing 51% attacks is crucial for protecting against centralization and monopoly in blockchain networks. By maintaining a decentralized and diverse network and implementing consensus mechanisms that prevent any single entity from gaining too much power, blockchain networks can preserve their core values and advantages and promote a fair and open ecosystem.

Conclusion

Preventing 51% attacks is not only important for the security and integrity of blockchain networks but also for the growth and adoption of blockchain technology. By ensuring security and trust, promoting innovation and investment, and protecting against centralization and monopoly, blockchain networks can realize their full potential and offer a decentralized, transparent, and secure environment for various applications and services. Therefore, preventing 51% attacks should be a top priority for blockchain developers, users, and stakeholders, and this chapter has provided an overview of why this is so crucial.

Chapter 4: "Preventing 51% Attacks

Strategies for preventing 51% attacks

Now that we understand how 51% attacks work and the potential consequences of a successful attack, it's important to explore strategies for preventing them. Here are some of the most effective strategies:

1. Increase Hashing Power

The most straightforward strategy for preventing 51% attacks is to increase the hashing power of the network. This means that more miners are actively participating in the network, making it more difficult for any single entity to control more than 50% of the network's hash rate.

One way to increase hashing power is to encourage more miners to join the network. This can be done by offering incentives such as transaction fees, block rewards, or other bonuses. Another way is to make mining more accessible by using more energy-efficient algorithms, reducing hardware costs, or providing better mining software.

2. Implement Consensus Mechanisms

Consensus mechanisms are the protocols that govern how transactions are validated and added to the blockchain. There are several consensus mechanisms that can be used to prevent 51% attacks, including Proof of Work (PoW), Proof of Stake (PoS), Delegated Proof of Stake (DPoS), and Practical Byzantine Fault Tolerance (PBFT).

PoW is the consensus mechanism currently used by Bitcoin and other popular cryptocurrencies. PoW requires miners to solve complex mathematical problems in order to validate transactions and add them to the blockchain. This makes it difficult for any single entity to control the network since they would need to have significant computational power to do so.

PoS, on the other hand, requires validators to hold a certain amount of cryptocurrency as collateral to validate transactions. This means that validators have a financial stake in the network's security, making it less likely that they will engage in malicious behavior.

DPoS is a variation of PoS that uses a small group of trusted validators to validate transactions. Validators are selected by the community and have a financial stake in the network's security, making it less likely that they will engage in malicious behavior.

PBFT is a consensus mechanism used in permissioned blockchains, where participants are known and trusted. PBFT requires all participants to agree on a transaction before it is added to the blockchain, making it difficult for any single entity to control the network.

3. Implement Multi-Algorithm Mining

Multi-algorithm mining is the process of using multiple mining algorithms simultaneously to validate transactions and add them to the blockchain. This makes it more difficult for any single entity to control the network since they would need to control multiple algorithms at the same time.

4. Implement Centralized Failover Protection

Centralized failover protection is a strategy that involves setting up multiple nodes to act as backups in case the primary node fails. This helps prevent 51% attacks by ensuring that the network can continue to function even if one node is compromised.

5. Implement Network Monitoring

Network monitoring involves continuously monitoring the network for any signs of a potential 51% attack. This can be done by analyzing the network's hash rate, the number of miners participating, and other relevant metrics. If any anomalies are detected, steps can be taken to prevent a potential attack.

6. Implement Community Governance

Community governance involves giving the community a say in how the network is run and how consensus mechanisms are implemented. This can help prevent 51% attacks by ensuring that decisions are made in the best interest of the community and not just a single entity.

7. Implement Immutable Data Storage

Immutable data storage involves storing data in a way that prevents it from being altered or deleted. This can help prevent 51% attacks by ensuring that the blockchain's data is always accurate and tamper-proof.

Conclusion

Preventing 51% attacks is crucial for the growth and security of blockchain technology. While 51% attacks are not easy to execute, they can have catastrophic consequences if successful. Therefore, it is essential to implement effective prevention strategies to mitigate the risks associated with these attacks. In this chapter, we will discuss various strategies for preventing 51% attacks. These strategies include both technical solutions and community-driven efforts to ensure the decentralization of the network. By implementing these strategies, we can reduce the likelihood of a successful 51% attack, thus increasing the security and stability of the blockchain ecosystem.

One of the most effective strategies for preventing 51% attacks is to increase the hash rate of the network. The hash rate is the measure of computational power being used to mine new blocks on the blockchain. When the hash rate is high, it becomes more difficult for attackers to control 51% of the network's computing power. This can be achieved through the use of more powerful mining hardware, such as ASICs (application-specific integrated circuits), or by increasing the number of miners participating in the network. Another strategy is to use a hybrid consensus algorithm, which combines the proof-of-work (PoW) and proof-of-stake (PoS) mechanisms. This approach can increase the security of the network by making it more difficult for attackers to control 51% of the network's resources.

Another way to prevent 51% attacks is to implement multi-layered security measures. This includes the use of advanced encryption algorithms, secure network protocols, and multi-factor authentication mechanisms. By implementing these measures, it becomes more challenging for attackers to gain unauthorized access to the network or to manipulate the blockchain's transactions. Additionally, it is crucial to promote community-driven efforts to ensure the decentralization of the network. This can be achieved through the use of open-source software, transparent governance models, and active participation from the community. By encouraging a decentralized and diverse network, we can reduce the risk of a single entity gaining control of the network and executing a 51% attack.

Comparison of proof-of-work and proof-of-stake mechanisms

Blockchain technology relies on a consensus mechanism to maintain the integrity of its transactions and prevent double-spending. The two most common consensus mechanisms used by blockchain networks are Proof-of-Work (PoW) and Proof-of-Stake (PoS). Both mechanisms have their advantages and disadvantages, but they have fundamentally different approaches to achieving consensus.

Proof-of-Work is the mechanism that underpins the Bitcoin network, and it involves miners competing to solve complex mathematical problems. The first miner to solve the problem is rewarded with a certain amount of Bitcoin, and their solution is added to the blockchain. The miners then move on to solving the next block, creating a continuous chain of blocks that make up the blockchain.

The advantage of PoW is that it is highly secure, as it requires a significant amount of computational power to solve the mathematical problems. This means that an attacker would need to control more than 50% of the network's computational power to perform a 51% attack.

However, this also means that PoW is incredibly energy-intensive, as miners must continually consume large amounts of electricity to power their mining rigs.

Proof-of-Stake, on the other hand, is a mechanism that requires validators to stake a certain amount of cryptocurrency to participate in the consensus process. Validators are chosen to validate new transactions and add them to the blockchain based on the amount of cryptocurrency they have staked. In PoS, there is no need for miners to compete to solve complex mathematical problems, making it much less energy-intensive than PoW.

The advantage of PoS is that it is more energy-efficient, as validators do not need to continually consume large amounts of electricity to participate in the consensus process. However, PoS is more vulnerable to certain types of attacks, such as a "nothing-at-stake" attack, where validators may attempt to validate multiple chains simultaneously to maximize their profits. Another potential issue with PoS is that it can be more centralized, as validators with larger stakes have a greater influence over the network.

In conclusion, both PoW and PoS have their advantages and disadvantages when it comes to preventing 51% attacks. PoW is highly secure, but energy-intensive, while PoS is more energy-efficient, but potentially more vulnerable to certain types of attacks. Ultimately, the choice between PoW and PoS will depend on the specific needs and goals of each blockchain network.

Other prevention techniques, such as sharding and cross-chain interoperability

Apart from proof-of-work and proof-of-stake mechanisms, there are other prevention techniques that can be implemented to prevent 51% attacks. In this section, we will explore two of these techniques: sharding and cross-chain interoperability.

Sharding is a technique used to partition the blockchain network into smaller, more manageable segments called shards. Each shard has its own set of nodes and can process transactions independently of other shards. Sharding helps increase the scalability of the blockchain network while reducing the likelihood of a 51% attack.

In a sharded blockchain, an attacker would need to control 51% of the nodes in each shard to launch a successful attack. This makes it much more difficult and resource-intensive for attackers to carry out a 51% attack.

Another technique for preventing 51% attacks is cross-chain interoperability. Cross-chain interoperability refers to the ability of different blockchain networks to communicate with each other and exchange data. By enabling cross-chain communication, users can transact across multiple blockchain networks, making it more difficult for attackers to control 51% of a single network.

Cross-chain interoperability can also help reduce the risk of a 51% attack by providing more options for mining and validation. This reduces the concentration of mining power in a single network, making it more difficult for attackers to gain control of 51% of the network.

Several projects are currently working on cross-chain interoperability solutions, including Polkadot, Cosmos, and Chainlink. These solutions aim to create a seamless network of interconnected blockchains that can communicate with each other, providing users with greater flexibility and security.

Overall, sharding and cross-chain interoperability are promising techniques for preventing 51% attacks. By implementing these solutions, blockchain networks can increase their scalability and reduce the likelihood of a successful attack. However, it's important to note that these solutions are still in development, and more research is needed to fully evaluate their effectiveness.

Conclusion

Summary of key takeaways

After examining the various aspects of 51% attacks on blockchain technology, several key takeaways emerge. Firstly, 51% attacks are a significant threat to the security and integrity of the blockchain network. These attacks can result in the manipulation of transactions, double-spending, and ultimately the loss of trust in the blockchain ecosystem. Secondly, 51% attacks can have significant financial repercussions for investors, miners, and developers. Thirdly, the prevention of 51% attacks is crucial for the continued growth and adoption of blockchain technology.

One of the most effective prevention strategies for 51% attacks is the implementation of a proof-of-stake consensus mechanism. Compared to proof-of-work, proof-of-stake reduces the computational power required for mining, making it more difficult and costly for attackers to obtain a 51% majority. Other prevention techniques, such as sharding and cross-chain interoperability, can also reduce the impact of 51% attacks by increasing the number of nodes involved in the network and reducing the concentration of power among a small group of miners.

It is also essential to note that the prevention of 51% attacks is not a one-time process but requires ongoing monitoring and adjustment. As new vulnerabilities and attack vectors emerge, blockchain developers must remain vigilant and develop new strategies for prevention.

In conclusion, 51% attacks represent a significant threat to the security and stability of the blockchain ecosystem. To prevent 51% attacks, developers must implement a combination of prevention techniques, including proof-of-stake consensus mechanisms, sharding, and cross-chain interoperability. By taking a proactive and ongoing approach to prevention, the blockchain ecosystem can continue to grow and thrive in a secure and trustworthy environment.

Call to action for preventing 51% attacks

As the use of blockchain technology continues to grow and evolve, it is imperative that measures are taken to prevent 51% attacks. These attacks can cause significant damage to the integrity and security of a blockchain ecosystem, potentially leading to the loss of funds and a loss of trust in the technology.

To prevent 51% attacks, it is essential to have a comprehensive understanding of the technical aspects of the blockchain and the vulnerabilities that attackers may exploit. As discussed in this paper, one of the most effective methods for preventing 51% attacks is through the implementation of consensus mechanisms such as proof-of-work and proof-of-stake.

However, it is important to note that there is no one-size-fits-all solution to preventing 51% attacks. Different blockchain ecosystems may require different prevention techniques, such as sharding or cross-chain interoperability. It is crucial to consider the unique characteristics of each blockchain and implement appropriate prevention strategies accordingly.

In addition to technical solutions, it is also important to emphasize the role of education and awareness in preventing 51% attacks. Users and stakeholders should be educated on the risks associated with these attacks and the measures they can take to protect their investments.

As blockchain technology continues to gain adoption and the value of cryptocurrencies and other digital assets continues to rise, the stakes for preventing 51% attacks become higher. It is the responsibility of developers, users, and stakeholders in the blockchain community to work together to prevent these attacks and ensure the long-term viability and success of the technology.

In conclusion, preventing 51% attacks is a critical issue in the world of blockchain. By implementing appropriate prevention strategies, educating stakeholders, and remaining vigilant against potential threats, we can work towards a more secure and trustworthy blockchain ecosystem. The future of blockchain technology depends on our collective efforts to prevent these attacks and maintain the integrity of the system.

THE END

Key Terms and Definitions

To help you better understand the language and concepts related to aging and older adults, below you will find a list of key terms and their definitions.

1. Blockchain: A decentralized and distributed digital ledger that records transactions in a secure and transparent manner.

2. Consensus Mechanism: A process for achieving agreement among network participants on the contents of a blockchain ledger.

3. Proof-of-Work (PoW): A consensus mechanism used in blockchain networks that requires participants to solve complex mathematical puzzles to validate transactions and add blocks to the chain.

4. Proof-of-Stake (PoS): A consensus mechanism used in blockchain networks that requires participants to demonstrate ownership of a certain amount of cryptocurrency in order to validate transactions and add blocks to the chain.

5. 51% Attack: A scenario in which a single entity or group of entities controls more than 50% of the computing

power in a blockchain network, enabling them to potentially manipulate transactions and double-spend coins.

6. Double Spend: A fraudulent transaction in which the same funds are spent more than once.

7. Sybil Attack: A type of attack in which a single entity creates multiple identities or nodes to gain control over a blockchain network.

8. Sharding: A technique used in some blockchain networks to partition the network into smaller groups of nodes, reducing the computing power required to validate transactions.

9. Cross-Chain Interoperability: The ability of different blockchain networks to communicate and exchange information with one another.

10. Merkle Tree: A data structure used in blockchain technology to efficiently verify the integrity of large amounts of data.

Supporting Materials

Introduction:

- Nakamoto, S. (2008). Bitcoin: A Peer-to-Peer Electronic Cash System. https://bitcoin.org/bitcoin.pdf

- Buterin, V. (2014). A Next-Generation Smart Contract and Decentralized Application Platform. https://github.com/ethereum/wiki/wiki/White-Paper

Chapter 1: "What are 51% Attacks?":

- Nakamoto, S. (2008). Bitcoin: A Peer-to-Peer Electronic Cash System. https://bitcoin.org/bitcoin.pdf

- Eyal, I., & Sirer, E. G. (2018). Majority Is Not Enough: Bitcoin Mining Is Vulnerable. Communications of the ACM, 61(7), 95–102. https://doi.org/10.1145/3212990

Chapter 2: "How do 51% Attacks Work?":

- Eyal, I., & Sirer, E. G. (2018). Majority Is Not Enough: Bitcoin Mining Is Vulnerable. Communications of the ACM, 61(7), 95–102. https://doi.org/10.1145/3212990

- Racz, P., & Vetro, A. (2019). 51% Attacks on Proof-of-Work Cryptocurrencies. In M. Christofides & A. G. Korfiatis (Eds.), Handbook of Blockchain, Digital Finance, and Inclusion (pp.

463-486). Springer. https://doi.org/10.1007/978-3-319-89399-0_22

Chapter 3: "The Impact of 51% Attacks":

- Croman, K., Decker, C., Eyal, I., Gencer, A. E., Juels, A., Kosba, A., Miller, A., Saxena, P., Shi, E., & Song, D. (2016). On Scaling Decentralized Blockchains. In S&P 2016 Proceedings (pp. 65-80). IEEE. https://doi.org/10.1109/SP.2016.11

- Delgado-Segura, S., Pérez-Solà, C., & Herrera-Joancomartí, J. (2019). A Taxonomy of Blockchain Attacks and Vulnerabilities. IEEE Communications Surveys & Tutorials, 21(4), 3653-3711. https://doi.org/10.1109/COMST.2019.2927288

Chapter 4: "Preventing 51% Attacks":

- Buterin, V. (2014). A Next-Generation Smart Contract and Decentralized Application Platform. https://github.com/ethereum/wiki/wiki/White-Paper

- Kiayias, A., Russell, A., David, B., & Oliynykov, R. (2017). Ouroboros: A Provably Secure Proof-of-Stake Blockchain Protocol. In S&P 2017 Proceedings (pp. 357-375). IEEE. https://doi.org/10.1109/SP.2017.47

Conclusion:

- Narayanan, A., Bonneau, J., Felten, E., Miller, A., & Goldfeder, S. (2016). Bitcoin and Cryptocurrency Technologies: A Comprehensive Introduction. Princeton University Press.

- Tapscott, D., & Tapscott, A. (2016). Blockchain Revolution: How the Technology Behind Bitcoin Is Changing Money, Business, and the World. Penguin Random House.

www.ingramcontent.com/pod-product-compliance
Lightning Source LLC
LaVergne TN
LVHW021054100526
838202LV00083B/5914